The
Word Whiz's
Guide to

New York
Elementary School
Vocabulary

By Chris Kensler

A Paper Airplane Project

Simon & Schuster
New York ● London ● Sydney ● Singapore ● Toronto

Kaplan Publishing
Published by Simon & Schuster, Inc.
1230 Avenue of the Americas
New York, NY 10020

For bulk sales to schools, colleges, and universities, please contact: Order Department, Simon & Schuster, 100 Front Street, Riverside, NJ 08075. Phone: 1-800-223-2336. Fax: 1-800-943-9831.

Kaplan® is a registered trademark of Kaplan, Inc.

Cover Design: Cheung Tai
Interior Page Design and Production: Paper Airplane Projects

Manufactured in the United States of America

September 2001

10 9 8 7 6 5 4 3 2 1

Library of Congress Cataloging-in-Publication Data

ISBN 0-7432-1099-9

All of the practice questions in this book were created by the authors to illustrate question types. They are not actual test questions.

Table of Contents

Introduction 5

Word Whiz Vocabulary Exercises...................................7
   All-Purpose 7
   Test Instructions 9
   English Language Arts 15
   Math 20
   Social Studies 27
   Science 37

Word Whiz Vocabulary Lists 42
   Test Instructions..43
   English Language Arts 45
   Math 49
   Social Studies 53
   Science 58

About the Author

Chris Kensler grew up in Indiana and attended Indiana University, where he majored in English. He has edited several test prep publications, worked as feature writer/reporter for a daytime drama publication, and written a book or two, including *Study Smart Junior*, which received the Parents' Choice Award. Currently, he is the editor of an art magazine, is married to the lovely woman who designed this book, and has some cool cats and a dog named Joe.

Stan Hattan is a figment of his imagination.

Acknowledgments

The author would like to thank Maureen McMahon, Lori DeGeorge, and Beth Grupper for their help in shaping and editing the manuscript, and Chris Dreyer for copyediting this book.

The publisher wishes to thank Karen Daley for her contributions to this book.

Introduction

Hi. My name is Stan. Stan Hattan. Please, keep your jokes to yourself. I have heard them all.

I am in the fifth grade. I live in, you guessed it, New York, N.Y. I am a baseball fanatic, a pretty good soccer player, and a vocabulary whiz kid. You name the word, I know its definition. Especially the words they use on the New York State tests. As a matter of fact, any word you are supposed to know by the fifth grade—I know it. But I'm not here to brag. I'm here to help.

I am here for parents, guardians, siblings, and teachers of elementary-school kids in the great state of New York—for everyone who wants to help students learn the vocabulary words they need to know. Let me be your guide to Word Whiz-ardry.

And if I can't turn your student into a word whiz like me, I can at least teach her a few more important vocabulary words—words that will help her in school, on the New York State tests, and in life.

Why Students Blank on Tests

Some kids mess up on tests because they don't understand the question, not because they don't know the answer. My good friend Larry reads all the time, but when the test asks the question "What is the best summary of this story?" he gets nervous, because all the answers look pretty good. My other friend Judith is a math whiz, but just last week she got stumped on a math problem that asked her which number is "greatest." She thought it meant which number was really, really cool, not which number was the "biggest."

This is where *Word Whiz* comes in. This book builds a bridge from the words your student does know to the ones used on all kinds of tests. Learning vocabulary this way makes it easier to remember and harder to forget.

Building a bridge is an active thing, so these are active exercises. They do not involve straight memorization–that's been proven to be a bad way for your student to remember words for anything longer than a day. *Word Whiz* exercises involve doing fun things like watching TV, reading magazines, drawing, and using one's imagination.

Lots of the exercises are also designed to become a part of your student's everyday life—as much a part as soccer or band practice. That way, the

WhizTip
Hey you—the adult who bought this book— way to go! Education is a team game. Just like Derek Jeter needs the rest of the Yankees to help him win the World Series, your kid needs a team to help him learn.

WhizTip
When you're
writing exercise
questions for your
student, always
give her three or
four possible
answer choices.

words can seep deep into the brain, so not only are you preparing your student for the New York State tests, but for all the big tests to come.

How to Use This Book

The book is divided into two parts—the Word Whiz exercises and Word Whiz vocabulary lists. The exercises cover words in five major categories: test instructions, English language arts, math, social studies, and science. Off to the side of the exercises, you'll see a series of icons. These tell you what "materials" the exercises employ—TV, magazines, the Internet, etc. Here they are:

Life   **School**   **Movie**   **Sports**   **Magazine**

History   **Imagination**   **News**   **Internet**   **Television**

On each exercise page, I also provide a **WhizTip**, a **WhizWord**, or an **On the Test** tip. A **WhizTip** gives more information on how you can help your student. A **WhizWord** is an extra vocabulary word related to the ones covered in the exercise. An **On the Test** tip shows you how the vocabulary word has been used on the state assessment test.

Lots of the exercises involve writing a story or a sample sentence. Not only will this help with learning the words, it will also help your student improve his writing skills. For this book, and for all schoolwork your student should:

- Write legibly
- Use complete sentences with appropriate punctuation and capitalization
- Spell the words correctly
- Use the correct verb tenses
- Use singular and plural forms of regular nouns and adjust verbs for agreement

The Word Whiz vocabulary lists at the back of the book have "everyday" definitions for the most important words. If your student hasn't heard of some of these words yet, don't panic! It's possible he hasn't made it to that stage in his curriculum yet. If you are working with a second or third grader, just make sure you discuss the words he doesn't know. That way he'll be getting a little jump-start for when they start using these words on a regular basis in class.

But enough of my yakkin'—let's boogie.

All-Purpose
WhizCards: Part I

In this age of computers, the Internet, and the Sony PlayStation, it's hard to believe that one of the best ways to review words is still the old 3 x 5 flashcard. I keep waiting for Nintendo to come out with something on the Gameboy to replace flashcards, but it hasn't happened yet.

Flashcards work for a few reasons. Reason 1: By writing down the word and its definition on the card, your student's brain has a better chance of storing it than it does simply by reading the word. Reason 2: Flashcards are a good way to whittle down a group of words to the ones your student is really having trouble with. If she starts out with 100 flashcards and after a couple run-throughs is only having trouble with 30 of them, you both know which words to focus on. Reason 3: They are portable. Your student can take them anywhere anytime. A few minutes of review on the way to church, dinner out, or a baseball card signing quickly start to add up.

MAKING WHIZCARDS EXERCISE
Get a pack of colorful index cards. Choose one color and one of the five categories of vocabulary words in this book (Test Instructions, English Language Arts, Math, Social Studies, and Science). It can be a subject you are both interested in or a subject in which your student needs to build her confidence.

Have your student print the WhizWord in large, legible letters on one side of an index card. Talk about the word. Have your student use it in a sentence. Try to think of clues or tricks she can use to remember it. Now you (the adult) write the definition and any clues or sentences your student came up with on the reverse side. (Use your best handwriting like they taught you in school all those years ago!)

Try to make 20-25 WhizCards a day, completing one subject before moving on to the next, until you have a complete set of WhizCards. (You can do more if your student is enjoying herself, fewer if she is getting stressed.)

By making these WhizCards, you will automatically improve your student's familiarity and comfort with a lot of new words. You will also know which words (and subjects) she needs the most work on. And, most importantly, you will be able to play all of the cool games on the next page.

WhizTip

It is extremely important for you to praise your student for his progress and, if possible, set up an awards system for this exercise. (My dad gives me baseball cards.) Make it something he looks forward to, not a chore.

All-Purpose

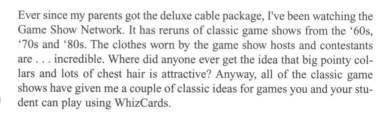

WhizCards: Part II

Ever since my parents got the deluxe cable package, I've been watching the Game Show Network. It has reruns of classic game shows from the '60s, '70s and '80s. The clothes worn by the game show hosts and contestants are . . . incredible. Where did anyone ever get the idea that big pointy collars and lots of chest hair is attractive? Anyway, all of the classic game shows have given me a couple of classic ideas for games you and your student can play using WhizCards.

WHIZCARD GAMES

Guess Again!

You need 2-4 players (two on each team) and a stopwatch or egg timer to play. One person on each team picks five WhizCards. That player tries to get the other person on the team to guess what the word on the WhizCard is by giving clues, without saying the word. The clue-giver can—and should!—say the definition, and think up other hints.

Each team has one minute to try to get through all five WhizCards. For example, after the first round, the score could be "three words correct" to "two words correct" (3-2). Each team then picks five more words and the team members switch places (the one who was guessing is now giving the clues). You keep playing like this until one team gets 20 words correct.

But you can also play Guess Again! with just two people. If you do, see how long (how many minutes) it takes to get 20 words correct. Play the game regularly and try to beat your own best record. (Note: It's important to discuss the words your team couldn't figure out after each round.)

Whiz Draw

To play, you need 2-10 players, a stopwatch or egg timer, and a big pad of paper. (Whiz Draw is best played with one of those big poster-sized pads of paper, but a regular-size notebook works, too.) Divide the players into two teams. One player on each team picks out five WhizCards. That "artist" has two minutes to draw pictures that describe each word. The artist cannot speak or write any words! Keep playing, alternating between the teams, until one team gets 20 words correct.

Whiz Draw is the most fun when you play with lots of friends and family members, but you can play it with just two people. If you do, see how long it takes you to get 20 words correct, with you and your student switching every five words from "artist" to "word-guesser." Play the game regularly and try to beat your own best record, and discuss the words your student couldn't figure out.

Test Instructions
Approximating

Usually, when I'm taking a test, I'm trying to find the exact right answer. But sometimes, tests only ask students to find an answer that is **closest** to being right. For example, there may be a reading passage about a boy who thinks that trains are really neat. The question could say:

Which word is **closest** to describing how Roy feels about trains?

> A. sad
> B. mad
> C. glad

Now, the story may not have said anything about Roy actually getting happy or glad when he sees a train, but he thinks they are neat, so "glad" is **closest**—**closer** than "sad" and "mad" for sure.

The key to spotting these "Approximating" words is reading the question carefully. If your student rushes through it, he could become frightened when the "exact right answer" just isn't there!

A good place for your student to get used to **approximating**—finding an answer that is close, but not exactly right—is at dinner.

WhizTip

Your attitude is important. Pay attention to what your student is saying. Show her that you choose words carefully to convey a specific meaning. Show her that you pay close attention to her word choices.

PLAYING WITH FOOD EXERCISE

You will need a notebook or a piece of paper and a pencil for this exercise. (I suggest a notebook, so you can keep it handy for some of the other exercises in this book.)

Now, have your student look at his food. Ask him to think about what food is approximately the same as what he is eating. If you are having pot roast, have him think about what food is close to that. A hamburger is about the same as pot roast because it is made of beef. If you are eating spaghetti, lasagna is approximately the same as spaghetti—they are both made of pasta and tomato sauce and cheese (if you sprinkle some Parmesan cheese on the spaghetti, that is). Enchiladas are closest to burritos because they are both Mexican food. (You get the idea.)

Have your student write down what the food is approximately like in a sentence in the notebook, using the words and phrases at the top of this page. So, for example, he would write "French fries are closest to baked potatoes because they are both potatoes." Do this at every family meal, rotating the "approximating" words every night until he has heard each of them—and written sentences including each of them—three times (three meals).

Test Instructions

Probability

<u>On the Test</u>
**What is the
probability that
Mark will choose
the black marble?**

**How did Junior
probably feel
before the match?**

The difference between **possible** and **probable** has tormented politicians since the dawn of time. Is it just **possible** I will win the election, or is it **probable**!?!

But politicians aren't the only ones whose success depends on knowing the difference between a **probability** and a **possibility**. Young test takers are faced with tons of questions asking for **possible** outcomes of math problems and how characters in reading passages will **probably** think or act.

So, to remember the difference between **possible** (could happen) and **probable** (should happen), let's make believe your student is—the president of the United States!

PRESIDENT EXERCISE
For this exercise, your student is going to run for president. Get the paper and pencil ready! Now, have your student make an argument for four things she thinks are really important—the ideas upon which she will base her campaign.

I am running for president because I think it is very important for this country that . . .

1. Everyone be nice to each other BECAUSE that would solve a lot of the country's problems.
2. We spend more money on the space program BECAUSE the Earth is getting full and we need to start colonies on other planets.
3. Everyone needs a new computer with a faster modem BECAUSE we would save all that time we waste waiting for e-mail.
4. I get another hamster BECAUSE my last one died and I miss him.

Now write down one or two questions for each of your student's campaign issues, like:

- Is it possible that you will get another hamster?
- Is it probable that you will get another hamster?

Now have your student answer the questions, and give one reason in each answer. So, for example she could write:

It is not probable that I will get another hamster BECAUSE my last one bit my dad on the finger and made him howl like a police siren.

Just make sure you use all of the "Probability" words in your questions about her campaign platforms.

Test Instructions
Place Relationships

My locker at school is just how I like it. While teachers have called it "a stinking mess" and "scary bordering on dangerous," I disagree. To me, it is a work of art. And I know where everything is.

My math book and my gym socks are at the **bottom** of my locker. My homework and my notebooks are crammed in the **middle** of my collection of decaying apples. (Mom always packs me an apple for lunch—but I hate apples.) The **inside** of my locker is a perfect mirror of my personality—a misunderstood, sloppy genius. The **outside** is plastered with stickers of my favorite bands—Limp Bizkit and Kid Rock—and teams—the Yankees and the Giants.

Why am I telling you all this? Because tests often use words that describe where things are. Your student should become as comfortable with them when he is taking a test as when he is describing his locker. These are also the kinds of words that you just assume a student understands. And he probably does. But you have to make sure, because they are used very often on the New York State tests.

WhizTip

Remember! When you are asking your student these test-type questions, write them down whenever you can. Your student needs to see the words on paper, not just hear them, so she recognizes them on the test.

LOCKER OR CLOSET EXERCISE

Use your student's closet, bedroom, locker, or book bag as the subject for your questions. Get paper and pencil and write one question for each of the "Place Relationship" words. For example:

Which of the following is at the <u>bottom</u> of your bookbag?
A. a can of Spam
B. extra-credit science project
C. a two-month old baloney sandwich
D. a Nerf football

On <u>top</u> of which piece of your clothing did I find moldy pizza last week?
A. your sweat socks
B. your pajamas
C. your new white shirt
D. your solar-powered-fan safari hat

Answers: A, C (Boy was Dad mad!)

Do this exercise three separate times—I suggest once a week for three weeks—to reinforce this important vocabulary.

Test Instructions
Facts and Opinions

On the Test
**Which statement
is true about the
first Germans
who arrived in
North America?**

When your student is reading about stuff she likes, it's pretty easy to remember what she just read. For example, I'm a Yankees fan. I just read the biography of Yankees legend Yogi Bera, about how he caught Don Larsen's perfect game in the 1956 World Series and had a long-running feud with Yankees owner George Steinbrenner. If you ask me a question about that book and give me four answer choices, I'm probably going to get it right.

But let's say you ask me questions about something I find really boring and stupid—like Christina Aguilera. It is harder to figure out the **facts** and **opinions** in a story you have no interest in. How am I supposed to remember what her favorite song is on her new album? I could care less! However, in order to succeed on New York State tests, your student needs to be able to distinguish between **facts** and **opinions**, whether she is interested in the reading passage or not.

READING STUFF THEY LIKE EXERCISE
You are going to use reading materials that your student actually likes to get him used to separating facts from opinions, and to get him used to seeing the words *correct* and *true*.

Pick out a piece of writing that has both facts and opinions. I suggest movie, music, book, and television reviews.

Your student is going to:
1) Answer two questions about the review (that you will write).
2) Pick out one fact from the review.
3) Pick out one opinion from the review.

So first, you need to write down a fact/opinion question and a correct/true question. Here is one example of each:

Which of the following is the opinion of the writer?
A. *Digimon* is a good show.
B. *Digimon* is a bad show.
C. *Digimon* is going off the air.
D. *Digimon* is on too early.

From the review, which statement is true?
A. *Digimon* is really popular.
B. *Digimon* is not popular at all.
C. *Digimon* is a show about snails.
D. *Digimon* is going to be made into a movie.

Have your student read the review and tackle your questions. Then ask your student to identify one additional fact and opinion in the review. Do this with three reviews, or until you are confident your student is comfortable with the "Facts and Opinions" words.

Test Instructions
Labeling

My big sister Hillary watches reruns of a really funny show called *The Young Ones*. It's about four college students, played by a British comedy team, who live together in this disgusting house. In one episode, the student named Rik is sick of his roommates stealing his food, so he puts paper labels on everything. And I mean everything. A half a piece of pie, a half a can of Coke, a "globule of green mold."

This gave me an idea for a Word Whiz exercise.

On the Test
Be sure to title the graph, label the axes, and graph the data.

LABELS ON EVERYTHING EXERCISE

Labels *are* everywhere these days, including tests. Tests ask students to:

- Label parts of speech in a sentence or paragraph.
- Label axes and information on graphs and charts.
- Write titles for something they have read or written.

For this exercise, you need either a packet of Post-it Notes or a few pieces of paper cut up into small squares and some tape. Now, put your student to work. Start out easy. Have him write some labels for some household items (table, lamp, dog) and affix them to those items.

Now move to your bookshelf and magazine rack. Have him write labels that name the kind of book or magazine it is (fiction, dictionary, TV listings, entertainment magazine, etc.).

Next, pick a short article or story in a magazine or book that your student likes. Underline five words in the story and have your student label them as parts of speech. (Parts of speech include nouns, pronouns, verbs, adverbs, adjectives, and prepositions.) Do this with two more stories. When he has labeled the parts of speech of five words in each story, have him graph his results. Put the part of speech on the *x*-axis (the horizontal line) and the number of times it appears on the *y*-axis (the vertical line), like so:

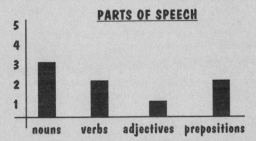

PARTS OF SPEECH

Have him title the graph. And you are done. Your student should now be comfortable with labeling and titling.

Test Instructions

Order of Events

On the Test

How many years
were there
between the
Battles of
Lexington and
Yorktown?

Some test questions work to make sure students can relate one event to another. Which events come **before** and **after** another event? What number belongs **between** 5 and 9 in this number pattern? The words are pretty easy to use in everyday conversation. ("I'm **after** you on the PlayStation! Have you heard the **first** single off the new 'N Sync CD?") But when your student sees these words on a test, they can get really confusing.

Using New York history can kill two birds with one stone. By learning her "Order of Events" words by reviewing New York history, your student gets to know the words, and she also gets to know a little more about her state, which could also help on a social studies test sometime.

EMPIRE STATE HISTORY TIMELINE EXERCISE

Kids learn a lot about their state in grade school. They learn the Dutch settled New York in 1626 and called it New Amsterdam. They learn George Washington's troops trained in what is now Greenwich Village during the Revolutionary War. They learn Franklin D. Roosevelt was the governor of New York before he was elected president four times in a row. They may even learn the Triangle Shirtwaist Factory in New York City was home to both an historic labor movement in 1909 and a tragic fire in 1911.

These events and others can help your student learn the words used to describe the order of events. A good source for New York State history is the New York History Net at www.nyhistory.com. The best NYC history timeline is the *New York Times'* 100 years of New York City history at www.nytimes.com/specials/nyc100/.

Pick a source and work with your student to make a timeline covering ten historical events. (Note: A timeline is a long, horizontal line with evenly spaced dots that indicate years or dates on the timeline.) When you are done, write six questions that pertain to the timeline, with each question using one of the seven "Order of Events" words.

For example, if you were using the *Times'* New York City history timeline that covered everything from 1938-1947, you could ask:

What happened <u>before</u> LaGuardia Airport opened in 1939?
A. Allen Ginsberg met Jack Kerouac in 1944.
B. Orson Welles produced his *War of the Worlds* radio broadcast in 1938.
C. Subway fares increased from a nickel to a dime in 1947.
D. V-E and V-J days put the city in a celebrating mood in 1945.

Answer: B.

If your student has trouble with any of the words, repeat the exercise with another timeline, writing questions that use only the "Order of Events" words she had trouble with.

English Language Arts

Sentences

Being able to write well is important in school and in lots of jobs, too. For example, my mom is a technical writer. She writes instructions and training manuals for a big electronics company. She has made it her personal mission in life to write the perfect DVD instruction manual—one that actually makes sense to a normal person.

So in her quest to show you how to use your DVD player, it is important she doesn't use any **run-on sentences** or any **incomplete sentences.** **Run-on sentences** get really, really confusing because they are so long and often contain too much information. **Incomplete sentences** are jarring because they are missing a part of speech (usually a verb).

It is just as important for your student to avoid using **incomplete** and **run-on sentences** as well. It is also important for her to be able to identify them on a test.

WhizTip
You can remember
interrogative by
remembering
the word
"interrogate."When
a person gets
interrogated by
the police, they
ask him questions.

OPERATING YOUR DVD EXERCISE

Grab a pencil and paper. For this exercise, you are going to give your student a mission: to write an instruction book on how to use a piece of electronic equipment. If you have a DVD, VCR, or CD player, go with that. If you have a stereo, TV, or radio, those all work, too. Even a microwave or an electric toothbrush will do!

Once you have picked a piece of electronics, choose a function. Start with an easy one, like "How to Turn on Your DVD Player." Have your student write a numbered instruction list using complete sentences and interrogative sentences. Like this:

1. **Check to make sure the DVD player is plugged in.**
2. **Is it hooked up to the TV? Check to make sure that it is.**
3. **Once you know it is plugged in and hooked up, press the Power button.**

Once your student is done, check her work for run-on and incomplete sentences. When you see one, mark it, discuss why it is either incomplete or a run-on, and ask her to rewrite the sentence as a complete sentence. (If you or your student are uncertain of any of these sentence types, check their definitions in the English Language Arts word list in the back of the book.) Repeat this exercise by writing directions for the machine's other functions, like:

- **How to play a DVD/CD/tape**
- **How to record a show/song**
- **How to set the clock/timer**

If your student comes up with particularly easy-to-understand directions, send them to the company that makes the product. Maybe it will replace the bad instructions with her good ones!

English Language Arts
Parts of Speech

Come close. A little closer. I have something important to tell you. Not only should your student learn what all these vocabulary words mean, he should also learn what parts of speech the words are.

No big deal—there are only a few parts of speech. It's not like we're dealing with Egyptian hieroglyphs—where every picture represents a totally different thing.

WhizTip

Grammar can be hard for adults, especially if you haven't had to think about it in a while. If you need to refresh your memory, get *The Elements of Style* by E. B. White, at your bookstore or library.

PARTS OF SPEECH EXERCISE

Have your student photocopy a page out of his favorite book or magazine. It can be *Harry Potter*, *Ranger Rick*—whatever. Now pick three sentences and have your student copy them onto lined paper, with a blank line separating each line of the sentence. Have him label every word on that page with a part of speech.

To make sure your student sticks with it, do this exercise with him, armed with this book (all the parts of speech in the list above are explained in the back of the book) and your trusty *Elements of Style* (if you need it.) When he comes to a word he doesn't know, discuss it and figure out what kind of word it must be. Here's an example from a story on the NASCAR Web site:

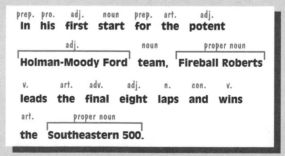

prep.	pro.	adj.	noun	prep.	art.	adj.
In	his	first	start	for	the	potent

adj.		noun	proper noun
Holman-Moody Ford		team,	Fireball Roberts

v.	art.	adv.	adj.	n.	con.	v.
leads	the	final	eight	laps	and	wins

art.	proper noun
the	Southeastern 500.

Repeat this exercise with three different pieces of reading material. Different kinds of writing use different kinds of words. Newspapers use a bunch of verbs and proper nouns. Fiction uses a bunch of adjectives and adverbs.

<u>Important:</u> Don't do all three sample passages in a row. You don't want your student to get sick of grammar. Do them over the course of a few days or a week. That way he will have time to learn the parts of speech at a pace that lets his brain absorb them. Spreading things out will also keep him from running away screaming!

Words Covered

detail, dialogue, hero, heroine, imagery, metaphor, moral, motivation, narrator, personification, plot, point of view, simile

English Language Arts
Writing Tools

I love to read. I just do. I also like to write my own stories. I won a young writers fiction award last year for a story I wrote about a cricket and his adventures in the Big Apple. I titled it "Chirpie and Vinnie." Chirpie the Cricket is the **narrator**. He has to find his city cousin, Vinnie, because their grandfather passed on (bass bait!) and left them in his will the map to the best vegetable gardens on Long Island. That's the **plot**. Vinnie becomes the story's **hero** when he rescues Chirpie from the clutches of evil Carl the Bluejay. They both live happily ever after, munching on the leaves of Farmer Ted's tomato plants.

Anyway, to write my story I used a bunch of the writing tools all writers use. Its important for your student to know what those tools are. Things like **narrator, plot, hero, dialogue, imagery**—they're all parts of what make stories fun to read.

WhizTip

If your student is unfamiliar with more than three to four of these words, do the story-writing exercise several times, using three to four words each time.

STORY-WRITING EXERCISE

Go over the "Writing Tools" words with your student to gauge her familiarity with them. Mark the ones she has trouble with. Use the word list in the back of this book to introduce your student to any words that are new to her. Write those words and their definitions down on a piece of paper.

Now set your student up with a pencil and paper or a new Word document on her computer. Give her 30 minutes to write a piece of fiction about her favorite subject. It can be about a superhero who does laundry, a pet cat who does good deeds for strangers, a cricket who visits New York City—anything. Supply your student with the list of words she had trouble with. Have her write her story, focusing on using the writing tools she didn't know.

The words should not be part of the story, but she should use them to tell her story. For example, if she had trouble with imagery and metaphor, she needs to use a LOT of imagery and a TON of metaphors in her story. The story doesn't need to win any awards, it just needs to show she knows what the words mean.

<u>Note</u>: You can also point out examples of these concepts when you are watching TV, in magazines that your student reads, and in movies. (If you point them out during the movies, keep your voice down.)

English Language Arts
Answer Words

Leave it to tests to make reading scary. Not only do us kids have to read things we wouldn't otherwise touch with a ten-foot pole, but we also have to explain what we just read! And they aren't easy questions either. The New York State test asks us to answer questions like "**support** your theory" or "**summarize** the third paragraph" or "**paraphrase** the writer's opinion of green eggs and ham." It's enough to make a young reader long for the days of *See Spot Run*.

But those simple times are gone forever. So it is important for you to make sure your student knows what these answer words mean. All of these "answer words" ask the reader to become actively involved with what she just read, which is kind of what this book does. The best way to get her used to doing this on tests is to get her used to doing it with reading material she actually likes.

FAVORITE BOOKS AND MAGAZINES EXERCISE

Ask your student to pick out two different pieces of reading material. It can be the latest *TV Guide*, a back issue of *Car & Driver*, Leo Tolstoy's *War and Peace*—whatever. Now you choose one short reading passage from each. Keep it short—no longer than one page.

Read each passage yourself and write down three questions. For example, for a *Soap Opera Digest* story about a hot young actor, you could write "Summarize why Ben Starrington thinks he will be the next Tom Cruise" and "Paraphrase Ben Starrington's acting technique" and "Support the theory that Ben Starrington is an idiot."

Have your student write a response to each question. Check them. In all cases, it is important for your student to base his response on details from the reading passage. His answers should identify the sections in the reading passage that support his conclusions. For example:

Support the theory that Ben Starrington is an idiot.
Ben Starrington is obviously a doofus because he thinks Leo Tolstoy is the actor who played the cowardly lion in the *Wizard of Oz*, he thinks Christina Aguilera has a better voice than Barbra Streisand, and his favorite food is wheat germ.

On the Test
Which one is the best summary of the story?

English Language Arts
Kinds of Writing

There are all different kinds of writing, but they can be roughly grouped into four categories: true stories, make-believe stories, drama, and poetry.

By true stories— also called **nonfiction**—I mean stories based on facts. For example, **biographies** and **autobiographies** are based on real lives. (I just finished reading a **biography** of the Yankee great Lou Gehrig. It was great.) **Essays** are also examples of **nonfiction**: an **essay** is a shorter piece of writing on a subject like "my favorite Yankee" or "what I did last summer."

Make-believe stories—also called **fiction**—include **fantasy** and **fables**. (The *Harry Potter* series is a perfect example of **fantasy fiction**.) And then there is **poetry**. One thing to remember about **poems** is that they usually rhyme, but not always. (I know, not much of a rule, but it's the best I can do.)

When your student is tackling a reading comprehension passage on a test, he needs to note what kind of writing it is. That will help him answer the questions about it.

WhizTip

The more time you spend in libraries and bookstores with your student, the more comfortable he will feel with books, reading, and using new words.

TREASURE HUNT EXERCISE

For this exercise, you are going to need books. Lots of them. So get in a plane, train, or automobile and get yourself and your student over to the library or your local bookstore.

You are going to be sending your student on a series of treasure hunts while you sit back and sip a cafe latte or thumb through a newspaper. Send him out into the library or bookstore or your house to find one example of each of the "Kinds of Writing" words. For example, send him out to find a book of poems and a book of plays. Depending on how well your student knows these words, you can explain what each one means before your student goes on his search. When he brings the books back, ask him why he chose each one.

Keep sending him out on these scavenger hunts until he has located each of the kinds of writing. (Note: He can also ask bookstore salespeople or a librarian for help along the way—Just make sure your student is the one doing the talking, not you.) As a reward, check out or purchase the book he likes best. My mom did this with me—that's how I got the Lou Gehrig biography!

Words Covered
**digit, even number,
negative number, numeral,
odd number, prime number,
whole number**

Math

Kinds of Numbers

WhizWord

ordinal number—n.
"First," "third,"
and "twenty-second"
are ordinal
numbers. They
are words that
show position.

My mom and dad have always been obsessed with gasoline prices. And with the recent turmoil surrounding high energy costs, their obsession has gotten even worse. My dad will drive for miles and miles to save 2 cents a gallon. I try to point out that perhaps driving all those extra miles and using all of that extra gas might counteract how much he is saving, but it doesn't seem to make an impression.

My mom has gotten into the habit of going to a website that has the current gas prices at local gas stations before she goes out to fuel up. This plan seems more rational to me. Unfortunately, she drives a big SUV that guzzles gas, so she is on that website a lot. Unless gas prices drop really fast, or my parents sell their big cars for subcompacts, trying to minimize the cost of gas is going to be a big family project for the foreseeable future.

GAS PRICES EXERCISE
The almost-daily ritual of pumping gas is a great time to work on "Kinds of Numbers" vocabulary. First, review the definitions of these words with your student. Then, whenever you pull into a gas station with your student in tow, ask her these kinds of questions.

Identifying Digits and Numerals
Ask your student to identify digits in the gas price. For example:

Premium gas costs $1.98 a gallon. Which digit in this price is represented by the numeral "9"?
(Answer: The digit in the tenths or "10 cents" position.)

Even or Odd?
If you take the decimal point out of $2.03, that makes the number 203. Is that an even or an odd number?
(Answer: Odd.)

Whole Numbers
Is $2.16 a whole number?
(Answer: No.)

Positive and Negative Numbers
To reinforce the difference between positive and negative numbers, have your student subtract the premium price from the regular price, and vice versa. For example:

If you subtract $2.13 (pPremium) from $1.89 (regular), what do you get? Is that a positive or negative number?
(Answers: -24 cents; negative number.)

Math

Symbols

It's important for your student to get comfortable with the different kinds of numbers. He should add them, subtract them, multiply them, divide them, group them, list them in order, etc. Once your student can do these things, he can progress to the next exciting stage in math—conceptual thinking!

Instead of using numbers that "are there" to get an answer, your student needs to realize that **symbols** can **represent** numbers, and have meanings all their own. So it is important for him to understand what the words surrounding **variables** mean.

THE GREAT UNKNOWN EXERCISE

Luckily, symbols aren't confined to math problems. They appear in "real life" all of the time. So, of course, that's where we will go to improve the understanding of these words!

Symbols

Symbols are everywhere. They are basically shorthand for words and phrases, kind of like the hieroglyphs used by the ancient Egyptians. Work with your student to come up with ten common symbols you see in everyday life. They can be logos for TV networks or sports teams, symbols used to denote money, letters that stand for a trademark—anything that uses a symbol to stand for something else.

Represents

Once you have collected a group of symbols, have your student redraw the symbol and write a sentence explaining what each one represents. Make sure he uses the word "represents" in his sentence. For example:

> The symbol $ represents "money" or "dollars."
> The symbol ™ represents "trademark." That means someone owns that name.

Variables

Have your student pick three easy-to-draw symbols. Now *you* write three math problems for each symbol (that makes nine total), using the symbols as variables in the problem. For example:

> 3 + ™ + 4 = 10
> What does the variable ™ represent in this problem?

Do this one symbol at a time. By working with symbols your student already knows, she will learn that symbols (like ™ and $, like *x* and *y*) can mean anything you want them to mean in a math problem. They are variables.

WhizTip
Make teaching your student different symbols **a part of your everyday life. Whenever you see a** symbol, **ask him what it means, and why.** Variables **become even more important in middle school.**

Math

Fractions and Decimals

WhizTip
Fraction and ratio mean the same thing. Your student can remember this by remembering the "tio" in each word.

What makes somebody "cool" depends on who is defining "cool." A bunch of soccer players might think the best soccer player is the coolest. A bunch of kids in an Internet chat room might think the one with the best home page is the coolest. A bunch of kids who follow the Yankees would definitely think the one who got Derek Jeter's autograph is the coolest. (That's me.) Cool is definitely in the eye of the be-cooler.

What does this have to do with **fractions** and **decimals**? Just be cool, I'm getting to that.

There's nothing truly cool about **fractions** and **decimals**, but coolness can definitely be measured using **fractions**. If your student is having trouble remembering the words that describe **fractions** and **decimals**, tell him to be cool, and try the following.

COOL EXERCISE
Get a pencil and paper. Have your student write down five television shows (or movies or bands or baseball players). Have him list them in order of coolness.

Now, write down a question and ask him to express the show's coolness with a fraction or a decimal. For example:

How much cooler is *Survivor* than *Friends*?
Answer: 1.75 times as cool. (That's just my opinion.)

Now ask two questions about his answer, using one of the "Fractions and Decimals" words for each question. For example:

1. Where is the decimal point in that number?
2. What is that decimal expressed as a fraction?

Answers: 1. Between the 1 and the 7.
                  2. 1 3/4.

Keep going until you can't think of any more questions. Like: How many cool castaways are there on *Survivor*, compared to uncool castaways? Express that as a ratio.

And so on. Continue this exercise until you have used each of the "Fractions and Decimals" words three times. (This may take a couple separate sessions. Cool?)

On the Test
What percent of students chose tennis as their favorite sport?

Math
Number Relationships

There are four math words that mean similar things and are easy to get confused: **mean, median, mode,** and **average**. Let's just quickly review.

- **Mean** and **average** are the same thing—it is what you get by adding some numbers together, then dividing by how many numbers you added up.
- **Median** is the middle one in a group of numbers. The same amount of numbers are above it and below it.
- The **mode** is the one that occurs the most number of times.

To remember these,we are going to use a couple techniques. First, let's use some word association.

- **Mean** "means" **average**, and **average** "means" **mean**. That's the way you remember those two are the same thing.
- **Median** is the middle number. Think of a **median** that divides a highway or boulevard. It runs right down the middle of the road. So does the **median** in a set of numbers—it is the number in the middle.
- **Mode** sounds like the word "most." The **mode** is the number that occurs most often in a set.

USING RECENT TEST SCORES EXERCISE

Now that your student has an easy way to remember which one is which, he can practice recognizing them. All you need now are sets of numbers. Test scores will do nicely!

Have him gather up all of his tests for a particular class. It can be for any class, but why not use math class as long as you're at it. Sort them from lowest to highest scores and find the values above. For example, I just gathered my math tests and quizzes we have taken so far. Here are my scores from lowest to highest:

34, 71, 83, 83, 92, 99, 99, 99, 110 (I got extra credit on that one)

Mean and Average	= 34+71+83+83+92+99+99+99+110 ÷ 9
	= 85.56
Median	= 92 (this test score is the middle value)
Mode	= 99 (this test score occurs 3 times)

Do this for the tests from three different classes. If your student's school doesn't give percentages, or you would rather not use test scores, you can also use: a baseball team's batting averages; the points or rebounds for the players on a basketball team; a quarterback's passing attempts and completions for a series of games.

Note: If there is an even number of test scores or numbers, the median is the average of the two numbers in the middle.

Math

Lines

The ability to define which way a line "points"—**horizontal, vertical, diagonal**—or how two lines are related to each other —**parallel, perpendicular, intersect**—is important on elementary school math tests.

When I think of how lines **intersect**, I think of Bart Simpson riding his skateboard through Springfield as the credits roll on *The Simpsons* TV show. If you drew his route on a map, you would have all kinds of lines.

SKATES AND SKATEBOARDS EXERCISE

Ask your student to think about where she goes on her wheels. Most kids these days have either a skateboard, rollerblades, scooter, or bicycle. (My mom never even learned how to ride a bicycle, but that's another story.)

Have your student draw a simple map of her journey the last time she used her favorite mode of transportation. If she can't remember the last time—tell her to get some fresh air! Then have her draw the diagram showing where she went. Here is mine from my bike ride yesterday.

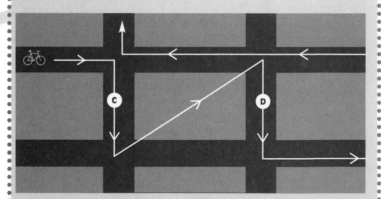

Now label some of the lines she drew and write three questions about the map she gives you, using the words above. Here's a sample question my mom wrote about my map:

How are lines C and D related to each other?
A. The are perpendicular.
B. They are parallel.
C. They intersect.
D. They are diagonal.

Answer: B.

WhizTip
If your student isn't up to going on a bike ride, you can have her draw a diagram of any kind of activity—like walking around a grocery store, or riding the bus to school.

Math

Polygons

A **polygon** is a shape with three or more flat sides. **Polygons** range from the familiar **triangle** to the exotic **octagon**!

There are a ton of them, and some overlap. For instance, a square is a **rectangle**, but a **rectangle** isn't necessarily a square. An **octagon** is always a **polygon**, but a **polygon** isn't necessarily an **octagon**.

If you think it's confusing now, imagine if you were 20 minutes into a math test and you had to answer a question about them!

On the Test

How many **triangles** would be needed to cover exactly 3/4 of this shape?

CAR SHAPE GAME EXERCISE

No, it's not about the shapes of cars, it's a shape game you can do when you're in the car. But this one could end up costing you.

The next time you and your student are in the car together, take the change out of your pocket or change holder and put it on the dashboard tray or in the cup holder. Start calling out geometric shapes. Tell your student to find a real-world example of the shape. For every one he gets right, he gets a coin.

Start with something easy, like "octagon." All Stop signs are octagons. Go to triangle, rectangle, trapezoid, etc. Tell him to look for the shapes in street signs, architecture, windows, and billboards. You probably won't be able to see them all on a normal drive, but if you play the game often, you will definitely end up a few dollars poorer, and your student will know his polygons much better.

The thing is, even if your student gets one wrong, or he just can't find a quadrilateral, he is still thinking and trying to figure out the shapes he sees. For example, you may call out "equilateral triangle!" and he may try to get away with an isosceles triangle. Use this occasion as an opportunity to discuss the difference.

Note: Want to spice it up a bit? Do "double or nothing" and have him define the shape after he has correctly spotted it. (This exercise is especially effective when a friend is also in the car providing some healthy competition.)

WhizWord

one-dimensional—adj.
Polygons are all one-dimensional. They have no depth.

Math

Graph Words

There are three kinds of graphs we will all be seeing and using for the rest of our lives. Knowing what they are—and how to read them—is important when taking all kinds of tests and getting around in today's statistics-obsessed world.

To remember which graphs are which is fairly easy.

Line graphs typically look like mountains, some rocky, some rolling.

Bar graphs typically resemble some sort of weird staircase.

Pie charts (also called pie graphs and circle graphs) look like—pies.

USING GRAPHS EXERCISE

Have your student use the three different kinds of graphs to explain how things important to him can be represented in graph form.

For instance, after your student sees a movie on TV or at the theater, ask him to show how much of the movie was about the characters, the plot, and the setting using a pie chart. Have him do this after every movie so he understands how pie charts are used. You can do the same thing with a situation comedy on TV. Have him divide a show by which characters the show focuses on.

Line graphs are typically used to measure something over time. So have your student trace one of his interests over time. If he has a favorite daily cartoon or comic, have him give it a 1-10 rating each time he sees it, and have him chart the results with a line graph.

For a bar graph, you could have your student chart the number of tests he has every week over the course of a month.

These are just suggestions. The point is to use events and activities from your student's life to reinforce how information is presented on a graph. Make sure he always labels the graph correctly, and make sure you ask questions based on the graph he has drawn.

Social Studies

Capitalism and Economics

The United States is a capitalist society. That means individuals own **property**, they produce **goods** and **services** at their jobs, and they are **consumers** of **goods** and **services**, too. The companies and individuals who are the **producers** of the **goods** and **services** try to make a **profit**.

Pretty dry stuff for a grade schooler! A good way to reinforce these words is to take an in-depth look at a company that makes a product your student can't get enough of. For instance—I just love Fruity Pebbles cereal. It tastes great and gives me the sugar rush I need to start the day out right.

WhizWord

supply and demand—n. When demand goes up, supply has to go up, too, or things get more expensive.

FAVORITE COMPANY EXERCISE

For this exercise, your student needs to pick out a product she really gets a kick out of. It can be Fruity Pebbles, a magazine, a video game, a bicycle—anything she wants. Once she has chosen a product, you are going to ask her to write five short descriptions using the "Capitalism and Economics" words in relationship to the product. I will use Fruity Pebbles as an example:

- Describe a consumer of Fruity Pebbles.
- Describe the producer of Fruity Pebbles.
- Imagine what it would be like to be an employee of Fruity Pebbles. What would your workday be like?
- What types of goods and services would the producers of Fruity Pebbles need to purchase to manufacture and sell their product?
- If you owned Fruity Pebbles, what would you do to make the company more profits?

If you want, you can have your student look up the company on the Internet to find some basic information—including the number of employees and its profits for the previous year or quarter.

You can also get more specific within each section. For example, for the consumer description, you can have her write down three characteristics that Fruity Pebbles consumers share, such as:

1. A love of breakfast cereal
2. A distaste for Count Chocula
3. High sugar tolerance

This is a fun exercise if you work on it together. Take your time and help your student with these new words. When you are done, if you think she could still use more work on them, repeat the exercise, but this time, *you* pick the company, and have your student help *you* write the answers.

Social Studies

Markets and Trade

Words that describe our economy appear often on social studies tests. And while your student no doubt knows that CDs, video games, and movies cost money, he may not be aware of the many vocabulary words that go along with everyday transactions.

A good way to have him nail down "Markets and Trade" words is to link them to how he takes part in markets and trade himself. For example, for the last year I have been mowing lawns for extra money. It's not glamorous, but it pays great. Anything your student does, or can do, to make money—babysitting, washing cars, selling cookies—will do. What you want him to do for this exercise is to think of his jobs or chores as a business partnership with you. I'll use washing cars as my example.

BUSINESS PARTNERS EXERCISE

Get out that pencil and paper. The most important part of a business partnership is figuring out a name. I call my urban car-washing company "Stan's Wash-a-Matic." Write the partnership name at the top of your page.

Now write down the things your student will need to get started. I need:

- paper towels
- rags
- spray cleaner
- rubber cleaner

This is where you get involved. Bargain, barter, and trade with your kid for the stuff he needs to get started. For example, I need a lot of Formula 409 to clean the outside of a car (two bottles), so I trade one extra night of doing dishes in exchange for a bottle of the stuff.

Make a list of the money and/or goods and services you have provided. For the things you have purchased for him, he will be in debt. Put a figure on that debt, either in dollars or in services (washing dishes). Once the business starts, he will have income and services that he can credit against that debt.

After you have shaken hands on the partnership, have him write a short business plan, using all the "Markets and Trade" words, just like any business partner would do.

Note: After he makes some money, take 20 percent of your child's income. Tell him that's the tax he has to pay for living under your roof. (Then give it back—you're just making a point!)

Social Studies

War

Your student will learn a lot about wars in her social studies classes. Most of the class time is spent on the Revolutionary War and the Civil War, with a little bit on World Wars I and II thrown in.

So it's not a surprise that war words show up all the time on social studies tests. Some kids—like my friend Larry—eat this stuff up. Larry can rattle off the generals in all the big Civil War battles. But students like me, with other interests like sports and girls, can have a harder time of it. So a good way to get the words to stick in our heads is to put them on something we all understand—a poster!

Posters aren't just for rock stars and sports heroes. Historically, many nations have used propaganda posters to rally their citizens behind their war effort. The World War II poster featuring Rosie the Riveter is probably the most famous propaganda poster, but posters have been a big part of fighting wars for years and years.

WhizTip
Your student's propaganda poster doesn't have to be about a war. It can be about anything she feels strongly about.

PROPAGANDA POSTER EXERCISE

Have your student create a poster for a conflict—it can be any war using at least five of the words above. Underline the words. Here's one I did for the 1991 Gulf War.

Top Golfers Golf in **Gulf**

Pro golfers Biff Conway and Fred Butlett <u>volunteer</u> for exhibition match in Iraq. Show <u>patriotism</u> and sponsor their match—pledge as little as $1 a stroke. The money you give helps buy the ammunition our troops need. Help our troops force Saddam Hussein to <u>surrender</u>!

Now, there are a ton of war words, so she probably won't be able to fit them all on one poster. Have her do two or three posters or flyers, then pick the one she likes best. Display that one to her bedroom wall or somewhere else in the house where she will see it every day.

Words Covered

checks and balances, citizen, congress, constitution, democracy, election, executive branch, judiciary, liberty, republic, unalienable rights

Social Studies

Government

WhizTip

Have your student check her constitution against the Constitution of the United States. See how her country's elections, checks and balances and rights and responsibilities compare.

As the 2000 presidential **election** proved, our system of government is a complicated one based on **checks and balances**. The two guys gunning to be top dog of the **executive branch**, Bush and Gore, had to fight in the Florida's legislative and **judicial branches**, plus the **judicial branch** of the United States.

Of course, it would be a lot easier if we lived under a monarchy and all we had to remember was "the king is always right, and what he says goes." But then we wouldn't have all these cool **unalienable rights** to do whatever we want, like watch golf highlights on ESPN II at 3 o'clock in the morning. (Please don't tell my parents.)

CONSTITUTION EXERCISE

Get a pencil and paper. Have your student name a country after herself. Now have her create her own Constitution for a democracy, covering these three important parts of democracy: elections, citizens' rights, and the government structure.

Preamble
Write a short summary of your constitution (you may want to do this last).

Citizens' Rights
Cover a citizen's rights using these words:
- liberty
- unalienable rights

Elections
Cover elections using these words:
- democracy
- election

Government
Cover the government using these words:
- checks and balances
- congress
- executive branch
- judiciary

Note: This is a hard exercise, so spend time with your student working on it. This exercise works best with both of you working together. To keep the fantasy going, ask her to appoint you as the vice president in her new country.

Social Studies
Immigration and Heritage

As you know, America is a country of **immigrants**. Only a small number of people can claim a direct link to this land. This makes words about **immigration** and different **customs** an important part of your student's education, because they are words about our country's history—especially in New York, the first American city many **immigrants** see.

But that doesn't make the words any easier, especially when they appear on a test. So to take the edge off this tough vocabulary, using famous singers, actors, and sports stars might be a good idea.

FAMOUS IMMIGRANTS EXERCISE

Have your student write a short biography of someone he is interested in who immigrated from another country. Have him structure the story with the following headlines, using the following words under each headline:

Celebrity Name
Home Country (majority, minority)
Some Customs of home country (culture, customs, tradition)
Why did the celebrity come to the U.S.? (migration)

For example, one of my favorite Yankees of all time is the pitcher Orlando "El Duque" Hernandez. Here's his story.

Celebrity Name
Orlando Hernandez is a major league baseball pitcher. He has a high leg kick. They call him "El Duque."

Home Country
He is from Cuba. When he was there, he was part of the Cuban majority. In the United States, Cuban immigrants are a minority.

Customs in Cuba
Some customs in Cuba are smoking cigars and dancing to Cuban music. Cubans have a traditional music I learned about from a documentary called The Buena Vista Social Club. It is part of their culture.

Why He Came to the U.S.
Hernandez migrated here in a boat. The reason for his immigration to the U.S. was simple. He came to play baseball because they wouldn't let him pitch in Cuba anymore.

WhizTip
Share newspaper
and magazine
articles about
immigration with
your student and
point out these
"Immigration and
Heritage" words.

Words Covered
climate, continent,
equator, fertile,
geography, hemisphere,
latitude, legend,
longitude

Social Studies

Geography

These days, the world is a global village. That means no matter where you live, people on the other **continents** are your neighbors. It's mainly because transportation (planes and ships) and technology (satellites and the Internet) are so advanced, you can get from one **continent** to another faster than it used to take to get from one state to another!

But wouldn't it be nice if the global village got a new neighbor? I mean, two-thirds of the earth is covered by water—even more if global warming keeps melting the polar ice caps. Along with the problems of overpopulation, this means one thing—we need another **continent**! I think putting one smack dab in the middle of the Pacific Ocean would be great.

CREATING THE EIGHTH CONTINENT EXERCISE

For this exercise, your student will be imagining what the eighth continent will look like. Graph paper is best for this exercise, but any paper will do. First, have your student draw a BIG oval with an equator line across the middle. mark the directions North, South, East, and West. That's the globe. Second, she draws her continent's outline and names it. Third, have her draw different regions on her continent. Fourth, using the "Geography" words, have her create a legend for the different regions. Here is an example of my continent in the middle of the Pacific Ocean. I have named it "Stanamerica."

Stanamerica: The Eighth Continent

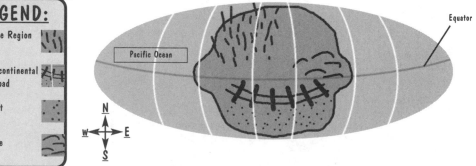

LEGEND:

Fertile Region

Transcontinental Railroad

Desert

Jungle

Equator

Pacific Ocean

N
W — E
S

Once your student is done continent-building, have her write a short story about how its geography is similar to or different from our continent's geography, using at least three of the "Geography" words. For example: The jungle just north of Stanamerica's equator reminds me of the rainforests I read about in *National Geographic*.

Social Studies

Rebellion

The United States began with a **revolution** and hasn't looked back. Revolt—both peaceful and violent—has marked our country's history since it declared its **freedom** from England. And New York has its share of rebellions too. From labor riots to the suffragettes' marches for equal rights, the Empire State has seen its share of **protests** and revolts.

When you are watching, reading, or listening to the news with your student, make sure you point out **revolutions**, large and small, going on around the country and the world. Explain the unfamiliar vocabulary words used in these stories to your student. He will undoubtedly come across these words in social studies class sooner or later.

WhizTip

What revolt or revolution does your student know the most about? The civil rights revolts of the 1960s? The American Revolution? Find out and compare notes.

YOUTHFUL REBELLION EXERCISE

Have your student organize a peaceful rebellion against something he thinks is unfair. Washing the dishes, bad cafeteria food, mowing the lawn, taking care of a younger sibling—you name it.

In order to gain support for his cause, he needs to create a flyer explaining why he is doing what he is doing. He must use—and underline—all of the words above in his flyer (this is kind of like the poster exercise we used for the "War" words).

Here is part of a flyer I put together asking my fellow Americans to boycott Jim Carrey movies until my dad lets me see them. Luckily, my dad was a good sport about it. (And his nose isn't really that big.)

JOIN THE BOYCOTT!

Stan Hattan begs you to <u>protest</u> his mean father, Dan! Dan prohibits Stan from watching Jim Carrey movies! For no reason!

WhizWord

justice—n. People organize **protests** and **boycotts** in an attempt to achieve justice.

Social Studies
Communities

**A community is
best defined as:**

A. a place where
people live and
work

B. a continent

C. a type of
map that lists
populations

D. a nation with
one culture

I have lived in two different places in New York. I lived in Margaretville, a tiny little town of 800 people in the Catskill Mountains until I was 8. And now I live in New York City. I really like both of these **communities,** but for totally different reasons.

Margaretville is a **rural** community. It's an hour away from Kingston, the nearest big town. There is one stop light in the town, and lots of people in town are farmers. I like Margaretville because I have a lot of freedom to run and play, I can go fishing whenever I want, and everyone is really, really nice and laid back.

New York City is, well, everyone knows what New York City is. It's probably the most famous **urban** center on the planet. I like it because the city is always exciting, there are tons of cool parks and museums my parents take me to, and I get to go to a bunch of Yankees and Mets games in the summer.

DESCRIBE YOUR COMMUNITY EXERCISE
For this exercise, your student is going to describe the community she lives in. First, have her read the short descriptions of the two towns I have lived in (above), so she gets the hang of it. Then grab a pencil and paper and write the four "Communities" words at the top.

Now have her write a short paragraph describing your town. If it has urban, rural, and suburban sections, make sure she describes each of them. If it is all one type of community, have her describe why it is NOT the other two words. You want to make sure she knows the differences and similarities among them.

Note: If she is having trouble getting started, have your student write about her favorite thing to do in your town and her least favorite part of your town. That usually gets the creative juices flowing.

Social Studies

Citizenship

A few years ago I just kind of thought of myself as a Hattan. Son of Dan and Fran Hattan, brother of Hillary Hattan. But in the last few years, my teachers have been telling me in school about the fact that we are all **citizens** of the United States and important members of our local communities and everything. They also try to drive home that we have **rights**—things no one can take away—and **responsibilities**—like obeying traffic signs and not littering.

The more I think about it, being a **citizen** is really just like being member of a really, really big family.

WhizWord
respect—v.
citizens **of New**
York City must
respect **people's**
differences,
because our city
is made of
people from
so many
different places.

FAMILY CITIZEN EXERCISE

For this exercise, you are going to have your student describe what it means to be a good citizen—of your family. Families have rules and responsibilities a lot like communities do. So get a pencil and paper and have your student write down the following:

Rights	Responsibilities
1.	1.
2.	2.
3.	3.

Have him write at least three examples under each header. Work with him on the lists, talking about the difference between rights and responsibilities. Here are two examples from my Hattan List:

The Hattan Household

Rights	Responsibilities
1. Eat three meals a day	1. Take out the trash on Tuesdays, Thursdays, and Saturdays

When you are done, have him compare being a "citizen" of your family to being a "citizen" of one of his friend's families. What kinds of different rights and responsibilities do the two different communities have?

Social Studies

Exploration

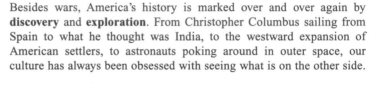

WhizWord

inhabitants—n.
The people who
live somewhere
already. After
your student has
written her
book, have her
write an epilogue
from the
"discoveree's"
point of view.

Besides wars, America's history is marked over and over again by **discovery** and **exploration**. From Christopher Columbus sailing from Spain to what he thought was India, to the westward expansion of American settlers, to astronauts poking around in outer space, our culture has always been obsessed with seeing what is on the other side.

So, many tests include questions about **discovery** and **exploration**. You don't want your student stumbling over "Exploration" words as she searches for the right answers, do ya? I thought not. Now, most of these words are pretty easy, so I am going to suggest a really fun exercise that will challenge your student's imagination as she learns the word.

CLIFFHANGERS EXERCISE

Have your student write a serialized story about discovering a new land. Have him end each story with a cliffhanger—an event that happens right at the end of the chapter that makes you want to turn the page, Use the exploration words in the title of each chapter, in this order.

> Chapter 1: Explore
> Chapter 2: Navigate
> Chapter 3: Discover
> Chapter 4: Colonize

For example, the first chapter of my story is called "Derek Jeter Explores Shortstop Beach." The last paragraph has him choosing between entering a dark cave to look for a magic talking baseball mit OR taking advantage of some prime tanning hours on the beach. (Hint: He chooses the cave.)

Science

Biology

Did you know that a species of yellow moths turned gray when a coal-burning factory moved nearby? And it wasn't because they were covered with soot—it was because they needed to blend into their surroundings. When their surroundings were covered in soot, the moths that looked most like soot were able to hide from the birds. The others got eaten. In just a few years, all the yellow moths got eaten, and the gray moths lived and reproduced.

It's called "natural selection" and "survival of the fittest." I learned it in biology class. Your student will need to know words like **inherited** and **acquired** and **traits** in order to understand these concepts.

WhizTip
Is your student especially interested in a particular kind of animal or dinosaur? Have him write a short essay tracing its lineage.

IF TWO CELEBRITIES HAD A KID EXERCISE
Have you ever seen those "separated at birth" features in magazines and newspapers, where they show two celebrities who look almost identical? The most famous one is where they show Mick Jagger from the Rolling Stones and Barney Fife from *The Andy Griffith Show* right next to each other—and you cannot tell the difference. It is so funny.

Well, this exercise is similar, except we are going to imagine what traits a child of two celebrities would have. Buy a celebrity magazine—*People*, *InStyle*, and *Entertainment Weekly* have literally hundreds of celebrity photos. Have your student cut out pictures of two celebrities. Encourage him to find two celebrities who are more different than they are alike. For instance, I cut out of my mom's issue of *People Magazine* these two faces: tall and odd-voiced singer/actress Cher and short and odd-voiced actor/comedian Billy Crystal.

Now use the words above to describe their kid, and then write how these traits will help the kid survive in Hollywood!

Words Covered
camouflage, decompose,
diversity, ecosystem,
food chain, habitat,
interact, life cycle,
organism, population

Science

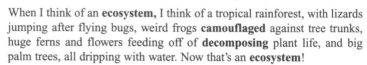

Ecosystems

WhizTip
One great way to
nail down these
ecosystem words is
to visit a natural
history museum.
Bring this book
with you and point
out examples of
each word.

When I think of an **ecosystem,** I think of a tropical rainforest, with lizards jumping after flying bugs, weird frogs **camouflaged** against tree trunks, huge ferns and flowers feeding off of **decomposing** plant life, and big palm trees, all dripping with water. Now that's an **ecosystem!**

But **ecosystems** don't have to be this dramatic. My family has a tiny back yard behind our apartment, and there are still a ton of **organisms interacting** back there. We get sparrows that eat the snails that eat the moss (a short **food chain**). Lots of flowers that my dad plants end up getting eaten by aphids, and weeds that grow as tall as small trees hide the chain-link fence that surrounds our little **habitat.**

ECOSYSTEMS AROUND YOUR HOME EXERCISE

For this exercise your student is going to describe an ecosystem that occurs near, around—or even in—your house. To start, get a pencil and paper. Have her pick an ecosystem—that's a system where different organisms all interact with each other. It can be a back yard, a nearby field, or woods. It can also be as small as a flower box or even the inside of an apartment.

Have her list the different organisms in the ecosystem: deer, flowers, possums, pine trees, grass, flies, mosquitoes, bluebirds, roaches, mice, rats, cats, sisters, brothers, etc. When she's done making her list (five to fifteen organisms will do) have her write a story about how the organisms interact with each other, using the "Ecosystem" words.

When she's done, have her read it to you and ask questions about the ecosystem she picked. If some things don't make sense, work on it with her until there is a final version she can keep and reread to brush up on these words. It doesn't have to win the Pulitzer, it just has to include all of the "Ecosystem" words and use them correctly.

Science

Evolution

America has spoken— *Survivor* rocks! Whoever thought of this TV show is obviously a genius. Gather 16 complete strangers in an isolated area, put them through a series of tests, see who can **evolve** with the situation, and have them vote one person off the show at the end of every episode. The one who **survives** gets a million bucks, second place gets a few thousand dollars. Everybody else gets nothing.

If I was on *Survivor*, I know I would win. I would form a strategic alliance with the cutest girl on the island, be very nice to everyone else, and win going away. I'd take the money and buy the latest PlayStation, a motorized scooter, an MP3 player, a . . . . But I'm getting off the point.

WhizWords

offspring—n.
resemble—v.
**Animals that
survive and thrive
get to produce
offspring, which
naturally resemble
their parents.**

SURVIVOR EPISODE EXERCISES

There are two *Survivor* exercises your student can do to learn "Evolution" words, depending on how big a fan of reality TV he is.

BIG FAN EXERCISE

This one's easy. Have your student pick his favorite contestant from any of the *Survivor* episodes. Have him write a short essay recapping how well his contestant did or didn't do, along with why she won or lost.

Have him tell how his favorite contestant was like an animal that has to adapt to survive and thrive in its ever-changing, scary setting.

NOT SO BIG OF A FAN EXERCISE

If you don't watch the show, you at least have to have heard about it. If not, check out the website online at *www.survivor.cbs.com/*. Once your student has a good idea of the rules of the game, have him pick a celebrity, and put that celebrity on the *Survivor* show. Have him write about how well, or poorly, the celebrity would fare against the other "no-name" contestants. Tell him to use the "Evolution" words to describe the celebrity's fate.

Science

The Environment

If kids ran the world, there wouldn't be such problems with the **environment**. We are natural **environmentalists**. For example, my school does that "Adopt-a-Highway" program—we've got three miles on the Interstate where we pick up trash twice a year. I also volunteer at the local animal shelter cleaning out cages, and when my dad sets mouse traps, I disable them.

Still, even though most kids care more than their parents about protecting the Earth, they don't necessarily understand the words that tests use to describe the **environment**.

ENVIRONMENTAL SUPERHERO EXERCISE

Most kids like comic books. So in this exercise, your student will be creating an environmental superhero—the defender of the ecosystem! Now, this isn't a new idea. That nature-loving super-hero Captain Planet had a comic book and a show on cable. (You can go to *www.turner.com/planet* to see what I'm talking about.) Your student may even have better ideas for an environmental superhero.

The first thing to do is pick out a name. I named my superhero "Habitattoo." He is covered in tattoos about habitats and the environment. His favorite one is of the recycling symbol on his chest. Anyway, have your student create a super-hero, and use the words above to say what this superhero does. You know—like Superman is "faster than a speeding bullet" and "able to leap tall buildings in a single bound." Habitattoo "protects <u>diversity</u> with the strength of professional wrestler" and "<u>recycles</u> more plastic bottles than a chain of grocery stores."

Science

The Universe

People are obsessed with what is "out there." The *Star Wars* movies, the *Star Trek* TV series, the Space Shuttle, and the International Space Station all prove it. Let's face it—the universe is cool. If it wasn't, there wouldn't be countless television shows and movies about it, and we wouldn't be spending billions of dollars to explore it. So, not surprisingly, space and the universe play a big part on elementary school tests.

But don't get sucked into thinking that just because space is so popular, your student understands all the space vocabulary words. Give him the list of "Universe" words above and ask him if he's familiar with them. If he knows them, great, watch the *Star Wars* trilogy on DVD together and move on. If not, let's keep playing make believe.

WhizTip

If you have cable, watch the Discovery Channel with your student. If you don't, get out your *TV Guide* and watch for PBS documentaries about space.

SUPERHERO SAVES ANOTHER PLANET EXERCISE

In the previous exercise, your student created a superhero who defends the environment. Now, have her write and/or draw a short comic strip where the character goes to another planet to save its environment. Use one word from the list above in each cell. One way for you to get more involved is for your student to write the strip and for you to draw it, or vice versa.

Here are the first two cells of a comic strip where my superhero, Habitattoo, goes to Saturn to save its rings from spinning out of control and smashing into neighboring Jupiter.

Word Whiz

Vocabulary Lists

This is not a dictionary! It is a list of 451 words important for grade school students to know. All of the words in the book's exercises are listed back here, along with other words your student should know when:

- **doing homework assignments**
- **taking tests at school**
- **preparing for and taking the New York State tests**

All of these words should become part of your student's vocabulary.

I have written one or two "everyday" definitions for each word, along with sample sentences and illustrations here and there for the toughest ones.

If your kid—or you!—needs pronunciation help or a more complete definition for a word, use a dictionary.

Word Whiz List
Test Instructions

according to —used in all kinds of questions, it means "as far as you can tell from" the information given. *Example:* According to this graph, how many nuts will the squirrel bury on Tuesday?

advantage *n.*—a benefit. *Example:* Give two advantages of using the railroad instead of the Erie Canal.

after *adv.*—following something in a series. The opposite of *before*.

approximately *adv.*—close, but not exactly.

at least—not less than; the lowest number possible.

at most—not more than; the highest number possible.

before *adv.*—previous to something in a series. The opposite of *after*.

best *adj.*—in test instructions, *best* is used all of the time. "*Best* answer" means the answer that makes the most sense; "*best* judgment" means use your common sense; etc. *Example:* Which word would best describe Lori's kitten?

best defined—this means when given a choice, it is the definition that best describes something. *Example:* A community is best defined as a …

between *adv.*—in the middle of two other things.

bottom *n.*—the lowermost position. Opposite of *top*.

closer *adj.*—the answer that is nearer than other numbers or objects, or more right than other answer choices. (Closer is sometimes used for proximity questions. See the definition of *closest* below).

closest *adj.*—nearest; most like. *Example:* Which nail is closest to one inch long?

continue *v.*—to persist. *Example:* If the pattern continues, what is the fifth number in the pattern?

correct *adj.*—right. *Example:* Write the correct number in each circle above.

estimate *v.*—to approximate. *Example:* Estimate the width of this line in inches.

example *n.*—free sample. *Free sample*: Rivers, lakes, and streams are all examples of bodies of water.

explain *v.*—to make clear. *Example:* Explain the steps you used to find the answer.

fact *n.*—something that is definitely true. *Example*: In this story, which of these is a <u>fact</u>?

first *adj.*—number one; occurring before all others. The opposite of *last*.

following *v.*—being the next in a series.

function *n.*—purpose. *Example:* What is the main <u>function</u> of the executive branch…

graph *n.*—a diagram that represents various relationships.

inside *adv.*—on the interior. *Example:* Write your answer <u>inside</u> the square.

label *v.*—to attach a name to. *Example:* <u>Label</u> the axes on the following graphs.

last *adj.*—final; after everything else.

middle *n.*—the center. *Example:* Which line passes through the <u>middle</u> of the circle?

mostly *adv.*—mainly; for the most part. *Example:* What is this story <u>mostly</u> about?

opinion *n.*—what a person thinks, regardless of the facts. *Example*: It is my <u>opinion</u> that the Knicks have had the best team in the NBA for the last ten years, even though they haven't won a single championship during that time.

outside *adv.*—on the exterior. *Example:* How many marbles are <u>outside</u> of the shape?

possible *adj.*—capable of happening. *Example:* It is <u>possible</u> I will grow to be seven feet tall, but it is not *probable*.

probability *n.*—the chance that something will happen. *Example:* What is the <u>probability</u> Bert will choose apple pie for dessert?

probable *adj.*—likely to happen. *Example:* It is <u>probable</u> that the Yankees will win the World Series at least once in the 21st century.

probably *adv.*—most likely. *Example:* What will Kevin <u>probably</u> do next, throw the fish back or eat it for dinner?

problem *n.*—something that is hard to solve. *Example:* Scarcity is a <u>problem</u> when…

represent *v.*—to stand for. *Example:* What do the stars on the United States flag <u>represent</u>?

statement *n.*—a sentence or group of sentences. *Example:* Write one <u>statement</u> comparing the two trees.

title *n.*—an identifying name. *Example:* Circle the best <u>title</u> for the story you just read.

top *n.*—the uppermost position. The opposite of *bottom*.

true *adj.*—correct. *Example:* Which statement is <u>true</u> about the first Spaniards who arrived in South America?

Word Whiz List

English Language Arts

abbreviation *n.*—a shorter way of writing a word. *Example*: *Mr.* is an abbreviation of *Mister*.

adjective *n.*—a word that describes a noun or a pronoun. *Example*: That's a *dirty* dog.

adverb *n.*—a word that modifies a verb, adjective, or another adverb. *Example:* That's a *really* dirty dog.

alliteration *n.*—the use of a series of words with the same first letter. *Example:* Simply said, Simon was seriously sick.

antonym *n.*—the opposite of a word. *Example: mean/nice.*

author *n.*—someone who writes books, plays, speeches, or articles.

autobiography *n.*—a biography written by the person it's about.

biography *n.*—a story of someone's life.

capitalize *v.*—to make a letter uppercase.

character *n.*—a person in a book, play, movie, or TV show.

chronological *adj.*—arranged in order of when things occurred.

cliché *n.*—an overused expression. *Example*: What goes around comes around.

compare *v.*—to consider the similarities between things. On tests, compare is often used with *contrast*. *Example:* Compare and *contrast* the views of Writer A and Writer B.

complete sentence *n.*—a sentence made up of the proper parts of speech and punctuation.

conjunction *n.*—a word joining other words together in a sentence. *Example*: Bob *and* Shanyce wanted cookies, *but* their mom gave them carrots instead.

conscience *n.*—something inside you that knows the difference between right and wrong.

consistent *adj.*—staying the same.

consonant *n.*—a letter of the alphabet that isn't a vowel.

contrast *v.*—to look at the differences between things. On tests, contrast is often used with *compare*. *Example: Compare* and contrast the views of Writer A and Writer B.

describe *v.*—to explain, using details.

45

detail *n.*—a small part of a bigger whole. On tests, students are often asked to find details in a piece of writing that support the students' answers.

dialogue *n.*—the speaking parts in a book, play, movie, or TV show.

draft *n.*—the first version of a piece of writing. *Example*: Jill wrote a <u>draft</u> of her essay, then went back and wrote a final version.

essay *n.*—a piece of writing where the author gives an opinion.

evidence *n.*—the proof that something happened.

exclamation *n.*—something said strongly and loudly. In writing, an <u>exclamation</u> is expressed with an exclamation point!

fable *n.*—a story that uses characters to teach a lesson. *Example*: Aesop's <u>fables</u>.

fact *n.*—something that really exists or that really happened. On tests, it is often used with "opinion." *Example*: Is the statement a <u>fact</u> or an opinion?

familiar *adj.*—1) common. 2) having a good understanding of.

fantasy *n.*—1) an imaginary story. 2) the opposite of reality.

fiction *n.*—1) a story someone creates using his or her imagination. *Example*: The *Harry Potter* books are works of <u>fiction</u>. 2) a lie or untruth. *Example:* Separating fact from <u>fiction</u>.

folklore *n.*—stories handed down from generation to generation.

hero, heroine *n.*—the man (hero) or woman (heroine) who saves the day in a story.

humorous *adj.*—funny.

identify *v.*—to name; to pick out.

illustrator *n.*—someone who draws the pictures that go along with a story.

imagery *n.*—the act of painting a picture (image) with words. *Example:* At the climbers' high altitude, the stars *glittered like diamonds*.

imaginary *adj.*—not real; "in your head."

incomplete sentence *n.*—a sentence that is missing some of its parts of speech.

index *n.*—the alphabetical list of a book's contents found in the back of a book.

influence *n.*—1) the power to affect an outcome. 2) *v.* to affect an outcome.

instructions *n.*—directions. *Example*: <u>Instructions</u>: Circle the verbs and underline the nouns in the following sentences.

interrogative sentence *n.*—a question. In writing, a question is denoted by a question mark. Isn't it?

interview *n.*—a conversation in which someone asks all the questions and the other person answers them.

legend *n.*—the explanation of the symbols on a map.

legible *adj.*—readable. *Example*: Make sure your answers are <u>legible</u>.

limerick *n.*—a funny poem where lines 1, 2, and 5 rhyme with each other and lines 3 and 4 rhyme with each other.

Example:
> There once was a plumber named Ray
> Who fixed seven toilets a day.
> He came home one night
> And found something not right.
> His dog had run off with his pay.

metaphor *n.*—one thing related to something else. *Example:* Her skin was *a cashmere sweater*, her eyes *two diamonds*, her lips *rolled-up $100 bills.*

modifier *n.*—a word that affects the meaning of another word. *Example*: Adjectives, adverbs, and articles are all <u>modifiers</u>.

moral *n.*—the lesson a story or fable gets across. *Example*: The <u>moral</u> of the story? Never turn your back on an angry bear.

motivation *n.*—the reason a character in a story does what he does.

mysterious *adj.*—without an easy answer; hard to explain.

myth *n.*—a story that explains the world or the universe. It usually involves gods, heroes, and adventures.

narrator *n.*—the teller of a story.

nonfiction *n.*—a true story.

noun *n.*—a word that names a person, place, or thing.

onomatopoeia *n.*—the use of words to imitate their meaning. *Examples*: *Buzz* and *splat.*

opinion *n.*—what someone thinks about something.

opposite *n.*—something completely different than something else.

paraphrase *v.*—to restate using other words.

personification *n.*—the act of giving non-human things human characteristics.

persuade *v.*—to convince.

phrase *n.*—a group of words that means something, but is not a complete sentence.

play *n.*—a dramatic performance.

plot *n.*—the events of a story.

plural *n.*—the form of a word that means "more than one." *Example*: The <u>plural</u> form of *gopher* is *gophers*.

poem *n.*—a composition in either rhyming or free verse (no rhymes).

point of view *n.*—one person's opinion or way of looking at things.

possessive *n.*—a form of a word that shows possession. *Examples*: baker, *baker's* / me, *mine.*

prefix *n.*—a few letters added to the beginning of a word that change its meaning. *Example:* dis- (*dis*ingenuous), ir- (*ir*retrievable), and de- (*de*claw) are examples of <u>prefixes</u>.

preposition *n.*—a word that relates a noun or pronoun to another word or phrase. *Example*: Ronnie ran and got help *for* Keith when Keith got *in* trouble.

pronoun *n.*—a word that takes the place of a noun. *Examples*: milk = *it*. Harold = *he* .

proper noun *n.*—the name of a specific person, place, or thing.

punctuation *n.*—the parts of a sentence that aren't words. *Examples*: period, comma, question mark.

relevant *adj.*—relating to the matter at hand.

revise *v.*—to change to improve; to amend.

rhyme *v.*—to link words that sound alike. *Example*: I tried to hit the rat with my bat. Imagine that!

run-on sentence *n.*—a sentence that continues on longer than it should, usually by using too many conjunctions.

scene *n.*—a small section of a movie, play, or TV show.

setting *n.*—the place a story takes place.

simile *n.*—an explanation that uses the words "like" or "as." *Example:* Her hair is *as soft as silk*.

singular *adj.*—relating to one of something.

suffix *n.*—a few letters added to the end of a word to change its meaning. *Examples*: –ness (bitter*ness*), -ly (like*ly*), and –ion (tens*ion*) are suffixes.

suggest *v.*—to offer for consideration.

summarize *v.*—to write a shorter version of a long piece of writing where you just cover the main points.

support *v.*—to give evidence proving or explaining something. *Example*: Please support your theory that girls are much better than boys.

syllable *n.*—one chunk of a word that makes up single sound. The syllables in *syllable* are *syl, la,* and *ble*.

synonym *n.*—a word that means about the same thing as another. *Examples*: *smart* and *intelligent*; *couch* and *sofa*; *road* and *street*.

table of contents *n.*—the listing of chapters in the beginning of a book.

title *n.*—the name of a book, story or other creative work.

theme *n.*—the subject for a story. In school, students are often asked to write a story on a particular theme, such as "What did you do this summer?"

verb *n.*—an action word. *Examples*: *run, spell, consider*.

vowel *n.*—the letters that aren't consonants, namely a, e, i, o, and u (and sometimes y).

Word Whiz List
Math

addition *n.*—the act of combining two or more numbers. *Example*: 11 + 13 = 24.

angle *n.*—the figure made where two straight lines meet.

area *n.*—the amount of space inside a triangle, rectangle, circle, etc.

arrange *v.*—to put in order.

average *n.*—the number you get by adding two or more numbers, then dividing by how many numbers you added up. *Example:* The <u>average</u> of the numbers 4, 6, 8, and 10 is 7. (4 + 6 + 8 + 10 = 28. 28 ÷ 4 = 7.)

axes *n.*—the plural form of "axis." <u>Axes</u> are the horizontal and vertical lines that make up a graph. They are usually (but not always) named the *x*-axis and *y*-axis.

balance *n.*—what is left over; the remainder.

bar graph *n.*—a graph that uses rectangles ("bars") to indicate quantity, with one quantity measured on the *x*-axis and the other on the *y*-axis.

circle *n.*—a perfectly round shape.

circumference *n.*—the length of the boundary of a circle.

collect *v.*—to bring together in one place.

combine *v.*—to add together.

congruent *adj.*—usually used with triangles, means having the same shape. *Example*: If you lay one <u>congruent</u> triangle on top of another, they match exactly.

connect *v.*—to join together. *Example*: <u>Connect</u> the dots on this graph.

coordinates *n.*—two numbers that show the position of a point in a graph or on a plane.

cube *n.*—an object with six square faces, all the same size. *Example*: A sugar <u>cube</u>.

data *n.*—the facts and figures in a math problem.

decimal *n.*—1) a different way to write a fraction. 2) the part after the period in a number. *Examples*: .<u>20</u>, 3.<u>45</u>, –10.<u>5</u>

decimal point *n.*—a period dividing whole numbers from parts of whole numbers (decimals).

denominator *n.*—the number on the bottom of a fraction; the divisor.

diagonal *n.*—the line slanting from one corner to another corner of a 4-sided figure.

diagram *n.*—a schematic that describes with pictures how something works.

diameter *n.*—the distance across the center of a circle.

digit *n.*—1, 2, 3, 4, 5, 6, 7, 8, 9, and 0 are digits.

dimensions *n.*—the length, width, and height of something.

distance *n.*—the length between two points or things.

dividend *n.*—a number to be divided by another; the number on the top in a fraction.

division *n.*—the act of "cutting" one number with another. *Example*: $4 ÷ 2 = 2$.

divisor *n.*—the number that is divided into the dividend.

double *v.*—to multiply by two.

dozen *n.*—a group of 12.

equal *adj.*—the same.

equilateral triangle *n.*—a triangle with all three sides the same length.

equation *n.*—1) a "math sentence." 2) a math statement where two quantities are equal to each other. *Example*: $2 \times 4 = 8$.

equivalent *adj.*—the same.

estimate *v.*—1) to guess; to come as close as possible to the real answer. 2) *n.* an educated guess.

even number *n.*—a number that divides by two evenly (no remainder). *Examples*: 2, 4, 6, 18, 20, 22.

experiment *n.*—one way to find out if something is true or false

extend *v.*—to make longer or bigger; to continue.

faces *n.*—the flat sides of a three-dimensional figure like a cube or a pyramid.

fraction *n.*—1) two numbers with a line between them. 2) part of whole number. *Examples*: 1/2, 5/4, 1/6.

factor *n.*—1) the numbers that are multiplied together to get a product. 2, 7, 14, and 1 are the factors of 14. 2) *v.* to break down a number into its factors.

graph *n.*—a chart that shows number relationships, usually with an *x*-axis and a *y*-axis.

height *n.*—how tall something is.

histogram *n.*—a special type of bar graph where the width of the bars can be different.

horizontal *adj.*—going left to right (or right to left).

intersect *v.*—to cross. *Example*: When two streets cross each other, they <u>intersect</u>.

isosceles triangle *n.*—a triangle with two sides of equal length.

label *v.*—in math, it means to name parts of a graph. Tests often ask students to <u>label</u> the axes.

length *n.*—the distance between a beginning and an end.

line graph *n.*—a graph where points are connected with a line. Usually looks like a mountain or hill, or slopes up or down.

mass *n.*—the size and the bulk of something.

mean *n.*—the average of a group of numbers. (See the definition of

equilateral
triangle

isosceles
triangle

average for an example.)

median *n.*—the middle one in a group of numbers, so the same number of numbers are above and below it.

mode *n.*—in a group of numbers, the one that occurs the most number of times.

multiple *n.*—it's a number that is one number multiplied a certain number of times, leaving no remainder. *Example*: 27 is a <u>multiple</u> of 3 (3 x 3 x 3). 16 is a <u>multiple</u> of 2 (2 x 2 x 2 x 2).

multiplication *n.*—the addition of numbers together a bunch of times. *Example*: 3 x 5 means adding 3 to itself 5 times (3 + 3 + 3 + 3 + 3).

negative number *n.*—1) a number less than zero. 2) a number with a minus sign in front of it. *Examples*: –4, –23.3, –400, –.4, –3/4

number sentence *n.*—a mathematical operation. *Example*: 8 + 4 = 12.

numeral *n.*—a symbol used for a quantity. *Examples*: 1, 2, and 3 are numerals. X, V, and I are Roman numerals.

numerator *n.*—the number on top in a fraction; the dividend.

octagon *n.*—an eight-sided shape.

odd number *n.*—a number that, when divided by two, gives you a remainder. *Examples*: 1, 3, 5…19, 21, 23.

opposite *adj.*—directly across from.

one-dimensional *adj.*—flat; having no dcpth.

ordered pair *n.*—the (*x,y*) on a number plane. (See the definition for *coordinates*.)

ordinal number *n.*—a number that shows position in a series. *Example*: The *third* hitter in an inning. The *eighth* planet in the solar system.

organize *v.*—to arrange in order.

pair *n.*—two of something. *Example*: A <u>pair</u> of shoes.

parallel *adj.*—two lines that never meet. *Example*: Train tracks are <u>parallel</u> to each other.

pattern *n.*—something rcpcating itself.

percent *n.*—1) per 100. 2) the expression of a fraction as a decimal.

perimeter *n.*—the boundary of a shape.

perpendicular *adj.*—intersecting at a 90° angle.

pie chart, pie graph *n.*—a circular chart where the pieces stand for percentages. *Note*: Looks like a pizza.

plane *n.*—a flat surface. *Note*: Think of "the Great *Plains*."

polygon *n.*—a shape with three or more sides.

predict *v.*—to figure out how something will happen. *Example*: If Joe eats four pizzas a day, <u>predict</u> how many he will eat in three days.

prime number *n.*—a number that has only itself and one as factors. *Examples*: 17, 23, 101.

product *n.*—the answer to a multiplication problcm.

pyramid *n.*—an object with triangles for its sides and a polygon for its base. *Note*: Think of the Great <u>Pyramids</u> of Egypt.

quadrilateral *n.*—a shape with 4 sides.

quotient *n.*—the answer to a division problem.

octagon

perpendicular

quadrilaterals

radius

radius *n.*—the distance from the center to the edge of a circle.

random *adj.*—in no particular order.

ratio *n.*—the relationship between two quantities. *Example*: 15 students per one teacher = 15:1 student/teacher ratio.

rectangle *n.*—a shape with four sides and four right angles. *Note*: Each set of parallel sides has the same length.

remainder *n.*—the number left over in a division problem.

represent *v.*—to take the place of. *Example*: In this problem, *q* represents the number 4.

result *n.*—answer.

right angle *n.*—a 90° angle. A right angle is formed when two lines intersect perpendicularly.

round *adj.*—1) having no corners, like a circle. 2) *v.* to estimate by going up or down to the closest number. *Example*: If you are rounding to the nearest whole number, 6.75 rounds up to 7. If you are rounding down to the nearest tens place, 112 rounds down to 110.

segment

segment *n.*—part of a line, usually marked with points.

similar *adj.*—sharing traits. *Note*: Usually used with *similar triangles*, whose sides have the same proportions.

subtraction *n.*—the act of taking one number away from another. *Example*: 12 − 3 = 9.

sum *n.*—the result of addition. *Example*: The sum of 4 + 5 is 9.

survey *n.*—a sampling of opinions.

symbol *n.*—something that stands for something else.

symmetry *n.*—sameness on each side of a dividing line.

tessellation *n.*—a mosaic pattern formed with small squares.

three-dimensional *adj.*—having volume and depth. *Example*: A sphere is three-dimensional.

title *v.*—to name. *Example*: Title the following graphs.

triangle *n.*—a three-sided figure.

twice *adv.*—two times.

two-dimensional *adj.*—on a single plane; having no volume. *Example*: A circle is two-dimensional.

value *n.*—in math, an assigned number or numerical quantity.

variable *n.*—something with a value that can vary (change). In math, variables are usually called *x* and *y*.

vertical *adj.*—pointing straight up and down.

vertex *n.*—the point where two edges of a shape meet.

volume *n.*—the amount of space a 3-D object occupies.

weight *n.*—the measure of how heavy something is.

whole number *n.*—an integer; a number that is not a fraction or a decimal.

width *n.*—the distance from side to side; how wide something is.

Word Whiz List
Social Studies

A.D. *adv.*—stands for "Anno Dominus." Also written sometimes as CE ("Common Era"). You count forward in "A.D. time," so <u>A.D.</u> 50 happened *before* <u>A.D.</u> 100. *Note:* <u>A.D.</u> precedes the year it identifies, but <u>B.C.</u> follows the year (see below).

adapt *v.*—to change to meet a new challenge.

agriculture *n.*—the act of growing crops and raising livestock. *Example:* An agrarian society revolves around <u>agriculture</u>.

allegiance *n.*—devotion to one's country.

alliance *n.*—the joining of nations or people to achieve a goal. *Example:* On the TV show *Survivor*, contestants have to form <u>alliances</u> to protect themselves from the others.

amendment *n.*—a change that corrects or improves something. *Note*: Most often used on tests to describe an <u>amendment</u> to the Constitution.

assemble *v.* —to gather together.

barter *v.*—to pay for stuff with other stuff, instead of with money. *Example*: Fred <u>bartered</u> for the Persian rug. He ended up paying the merchant two chickens and a goat for it.

B.C. *adv.*—stands for "Before Christ." Also written sometimes as BCE ("Before the Common Era"). *Note:* You count backwards in "<u>B.C.</u> time," so 50 <u>B.C.</u> happened *after* 100 <u>B.C.</u>

boycott *v.*—to refuse to buy something or do something in protest.

budget *n.*—the plan for how a country—or person—will spend its money.

canal *n.*—a man-made waterway that boats and barges use to carry stuff from place to place.

century *n.*—a period of 100 years. *Note*: The <u>century</u> is "one more" than the number. 1671 is part of the 17th century. 1945 is part of the 20th century.

checks and balances *n.*—the system of internal controls on the U.S. government. *Example:* The president, Congress, and the judiciary provide <u>checks and balances</u> on each other, so power is shared and regulated.

citizen *n.*—a member of a country or community. *Note:* Being a <u>citizen</u> usually brings with it defined rights and responsibilities.

citizenship *n.*—the condition of being a citizen of a country or state.

civil rights *n.*—rights due a person because he is a citizen of a country. *Note*: It usually has to do with minorities' struggles for <u>civil rights</u>.

climate *n.*—the weather of a particular region.

colonize *v.*—to start up a civilization somewhere new. *Note*: Usually refers to European colonization of much of the globe in the 16th–19th centuries.

commerce *n.*—the buying and selling of goods and services.

common *adj.*—relating to many, as in "the common good."

communication *n.*—the act of exchanging information.

community *n.*—a group of people who share a common bond. They usually live in the same area, but communities can also revolve around interests and backgrounds.

conflict *n.*—fighting. *Example*: Human history is a history of conflict.

Congress *proper noun*—the U.S. Senate and House of Representatives. *Note*: Congress is one of the three branches of the U.S. government.

consequences *n.*—the results from an action.

conserve *v.*—to save by using sparingly. *Example*: Conserving energy.

Constitution *proper noun*—the rules around which the United States was built.

consumers *n.*—the people who buy goods and services.

continent *n.*—one of the seven major land masses on Earth: Africa, Antarctica, Asia, Australia, Europe, N. America, S. America.

contribution *n.*—a gift. Something that helps a given situation.

cooperate *v.*—to work together.

culture *n.*—a group of people bound by shared customs, laws, and beliefs.

customs *n.*—the traditions and behaviors of a country's citizens.

decade *n.*—a period of ten years.

defense *n.*—the measures taken to protect something.

delegate *n.*—a representative; someone chosen to speak for others. *Example*: Elected officials are the delegates of the people.

democracy *n.*—a system of government based on the principle of equality where people hold the power.

discover *v.*—to find for the first time ever.

distribution *n.*—in social studies, it is the act of getting stuff from one place to many places.

document *n.*—1) a piece of paper with writing on it. 2) *v.* to gather evidence to support or prove something.

domestic *adj.*—having to do with one's home or one's country. *Example*: Presidents have to deal with problems both foreign and domestic.

economy *n.*—the way a country or community manages its resources. *Note*: In a market economy, private citizens own the means of production (companies, factories, and farms).

election *n.*—the casting of votes to choose among candidates.

eliminate *v.*—to get rid of.

enforce *v.*—to force to obey.

equator *n.*—an imaginary circle going around the middle of the earth, the same distance from the north and south poles.

ethnic *adj.*—related to a group of people who share a common heritage. It usually refers to a country (Irish, Spanish) or a religion (Catholic, Jewish).

exchange *n.*—to trade one thing for another.

executive branch *n.*—the president and his staff. It is one of the three branches of federal government in the United States.

expansion *n.*—the movement of a community or country to take over lands adjoining it.

explore *v.*—to search out new places.

explorer *n.*—someone who searches out new places.

export *v.*—1) to sell something to someone outside your country. 2) *n.* something sold to another country.

fertile *adj.*—able to produce crops or offspring.

financial *adj.*—having to do with money and its management.

free enterprise *n.*—an economic system where people are free to buy and sell stuff for whatever price the other people are willing to pay.

freedom *n.*—the ability to say and do what you want.

geography *n.*—the natural, physical features of a region.

goods *n.*—stuff that is bought and sold. In social studies, it is used in the phrase "goods and services" to describe the products of an economy.

government *n.*—the political system by which a city, state, or country os ruled.

hemisphere *n.*—one of the two "halves" of the world divided by the equator. *Note:* The northern hemisphere contains the North Pole, and the southern hemisphere contains the South Pole.

immigrate *v.*—to move to a foreign country.

import *v.*—1) to bring something from one country to another. 2) *n.* something brought from one country into another.

income *n.*—the money one earns at a job.

independence *n.*—freedom.

industrial *adj.*—characterized by heavy industry, like car and steel manufacturing.

inhabitants *n.*—those who live somewhere.

interdependent *adj.*—reliant on one another

invent *v.*—to create.

judicial branch *n.*—the system of courts in the U.S. *Note*: The judicial branch is one of the three branches of government.

justice *n.*—the act of laws being carried out.

latitude *n.*—the distance north or south of the equator, measured in degrees.

legend *n.*—the explanations of the symbols on a map.

legislature *n.*—a group of people (legislators) who make and change laws.

liberty *n.*—freedom.

longitude *n.*—the distance east and west of the prime meridian, measured in degrees.

loyalist *n.*—a colonist who remained loyal to England during the

Revolutionary War period.

majority *n.*—the biggest group of people. *Note*: In the U.S., the majority rules, but the minority also has rights.

memorial *n.*—a monument erected to commemorate a person or event, like the Lincoln Memorial and Vietnam Veterans War Memorial in Washington, D.C.

migration *n.*—the movement of a large group of people from one land to another.

militia *n.*—trained soldiers ready to fight at a moment's notice; an "on call" army.

minority *n.*—the smaller group of people.

modify *v.*—to change; to alter.

monarchy *n.*—rule by a king or queen.

motto *n.*—a slogan or saying, usually used for self-identification. *Example*: Texas' state motto is "Don't mess with Texas."

nation *n.*—a country; people who live on the same land and have the same government.

nationalism *n.*—loyalty and fervor for your country.

navigate *v.*—to direct something (usually a ship) from one point to another.

oppress *v.*—to prevent people from doing what they want to do.

patriotism *n.*—love of one's country. *Note*: Patriotism is similar to nationalism, but nationalism has a negative connotation because it means one thinks less of other countries, as well.

persecute *v.*—to treat people very badly, usually because of their race or religion.

population *n.*—the number of people who live in a given place.

preamble *n.*—an introduction to a document.

prejudice *n.*—thinking, for no good reason, that one group of people is better than another.

producer *n.*—in economics, the person or group of people who make the goods and provide the services. *Note*: In economics, producer is the "opposite" of *consumer*.

profit *n.*—the money one makes from selling something. *Example*: It cost Bette $3.00 to make that cake. She sold it for $7.00. That's a $4.00 profit!

prohibit *v.*—to not allow, to forbid.

propaganda *n.*—information that is supposed to make someone believe something; often an exaggeration of fact or just "one side of the story."

property *n.*—something owned. It can be land, it can be a pencil. Both are property.

protect *n.*—to defend against attack.

protest *v.*—1) to object strongly. 2) *n.* demonstration in the streets against something.

purchase *v.*—to buy.

ratify *v.*—to approve something and make it official.

reformer *n.*—someone who works to improve laws or customs.

Representatives, House of *proper noun*—one of two parts of the U.S. Congress. *Note*: In the House of Representatives, states are proportionally represented: the bigger the state, the more representatives.

republic *n.*—a government made up of representatives elected by the people.

respect *v.*—to hold in honor. America is based on people respecting each other's differences.

responsibility *n.*—something you need to do.

revolution *n.*—the overthrow of one government by a new one.

rights *n.*—as a citizen, something that is obligated to you. In the Declaration of Independence, rights of Americans include "life, liberty, and the pursuit of happiness."

rural *adj.*—pertaining to the country (not the city).

scarce *adj.*—in short supply; not enough of something to go around to everyone who wants it.

self-evident *adj.*—obviously true.

Senate *proper noun*—one of two parts of the U.S. Congress. *Note*: Each state is represented by two senators in the Senate, regardless of its size.

services *n.*—labor. In social studies, it is used in the phrase "goods and services" to describe the products of an economy.

suburban *adj.*—pertaining to an area close to the city, almost always a residential area.

supply and demand *n.*—a law of economics used in a market economy. *Note:* When demand for a product goes up, its supply must also increase, or the product will get more expensive.

surrender *v.*—to give up.

tax *n.*—money paid by people that goes to fund their government.

technology *n.*—things learned through science that we apply to the real world.

timeline *n.*—a special graph that shows events along a line, in the order they occurred.

trade *n.*—1) the buying and selling of goods and services. 2) *v.* to give something and get something in return.

tradition *n.*—a way of doing things, passed down from generation to generation. (See the definition for *customs*.)

transportation *n.*—anything that moves something from here to there. *Example*: Planes, trains, and cars are forms of transportation.

treason *n.*—the crime of being a traitor.

truce *n.*—a temporary fighting stoppage. *Note*: Wars usually have a bunch of truces before somebody finally surrenders for good.

tyranny *n.*—a government in which one person rules over everyone, and that one person is not very nice.

unalienable rights *n.*—rights that can never be taken back or ignored.

union *n.*—a group of individuals who band together to protect their interests.

urban *adj.*—an inner-city area.

volunteer *n.*—1) someone who does something for a good cause, usually without pay. 2) *v.* to join a cause of your own volition.

Word Whiz List
Science

acquired *adj.*—when talking about traits in science, <u>acquired</u> means learned. An <u>acquired</u> trait is basically the opposite of inherited traits.

amphibian *n.*—a cold-blooded animal that breathes with gills when it's young, and with lungs when it's older.

astronomy *n.*—the study of the universe.

attract *v.*—to draw closer. *Example*: Magnets <u>attract</u> some metals. *Note*: The opposite of <u>attract</u> is *repel*.

camouflage *n.*—disguise. *Example*: Some animals use <u>camouflage</u> to hide from predators.

celestial *adj.*—having to do with the stars and the universe.

classify *v.*—to group something. In science, animals and plants are <u>classified</u> into groups according to their physical characteristics.

condensation *n.*—moisture that collects as water or ice.

conduct *v.*—to help something go from one place to another.

conservation *n.*—the protection and preservation of natural resources.

constellation *n.*—a group of stars. *Example*: Orion and the Big Dipper are <u>constellations</u>.

consume *v.*—to eat or drink; to use up.

current *n.*—the flow of electricity.

cycle *n.*—a series of events that occur in order over and over again. *Example:* The changing seasons are a natural <u>cycle</u>.

decompose *v.*—to break down. In science, it usually refers to dead animals and plants <u>decomposing</u>.

density *n.*—the amount of something there is in a given unit of area or volume.

dissolve *v.*—to disintegrate into tiny particles and mix into a liquid. (See the definition for *soluble*.)

diversity *n.*—variety. *Example*: The Earth supports a <u>diversity</u> of living organisms.

eclipse *n.*—the blockage of light from the sun. *Example*: A solar <u>eclipse</u> is caused by the moon passing between the Earth and the sun.

ecosystem *n.*—a group of plants, animals, and environmental factors that affect one another.

eliminate *v.*—to get rid of.

energy *n.*—1) usable heat. 2) electricity.

environment *n.*—a person's, animal's, or plant's surroundings.

equilibrium *n.*—the balancing of opposite forces.

erosion *n.*—the process of wearing something away a little at a time.

evaporation *n.*—the process of liquid changing to gas.

evolve *v.*—to change from one thing into something different (usually, something better). The theory of evolution is based on the fact that animals <u>evolve</u> over time to better take advantage of their environment.

food chain *n.*—a series of animals and plants that eat each other; the cycle of life.

friction *v.*—rough rubbing. *Example:* The <u>friction</u> between tectonic plates causes earthquakes.

fungi *n.*—the plural of fungus. <u>Fungus</u> is not a plant or an animal. It is a third kind of organism. The most common examples are mushrooms and mold.

gene *n.*—the part of a cell that determines the different characteristics of an organism.

generation *n.*—a group of organisms all about the same age; one stage in a series starting with one ancestor.

gravity *n.*—the force that draws objects to the Earth.

groundwater *n.*—the water below the surface of the Earth.

habitat *n.*—the place where an animal or plant lives.

hibernation *n.*—the act of sleeping for the winter.

identical *adj.*—exactly alike; the same.

increase *v.*—to make bigger.

inherited *adj.*—from a parent; traits you are born with. *Example*: Big feet and hair color are <u>inherited</u> traits.

interact *v.*—to deal with each other on some level. Animals and plants interact with each other, and with the environment.

life cycle *n.*—the process of progressing from birth to death.

life span *n.*—the amount of time an organism typically lives. A dog's <u>life span</u> is about ten years.

lunar *adj.*—having to do with the moon.

magnetic *adj.*—having the ability to attract other things.

mammal *n.*—a warm-blooded animal, usually with hair, that gives birth to live offspring.

manufacture *v.*—to make. In science, it usually refers to organisms <u>manufacturing</u> the substances they need to live.

nutrients *n.*—the parts of food that provide the nutrition for an organism.

observe *v.*—to watch closely.

offspring *n.*—the "children" of plants and animals.

organism *n.*—a living thing. *Examples*: Plants, animals, and fungi are all <u>organisms</u>.

population *n.*—the number of one kind of organism in a given habitat.

precipitation *n.*—rain, snow, sleet, or hail.

predator *n.*—an animal that hunts other animals for food.

prey *n.*—the animal or animals a predator hunts for food.

properties *n.*—attributes.

protect *v.*—to keep from harm.

recycle *v.*—to use again.

renewable *adj.*—able to be used again or replaced by new growth. *Example*: Trees are <u>renewable</u> resources because you can always grow new ones.

reproduction *n.*—the act of producing offspring.

reptile *n.*—a cold-blooded animal that breathes with lungs and is usually covered with scales.

resemble *v.*—to look the same as. A parent's offspring usually <u>resemble</u> the parent.

resource *n.*—something used to achieve wealth or health.

runoff *n.*—rain that doesn't get soaked up by the soil.

season *n.*—one of the four natural periods of the year: spring, summer, winter, and fall.

shelter *n.*—a protective dwelling.

solar system *n.*—the sun, the group of planets, and the other heavenly bodies surrounding our sun. *Note: solar means sun.*

soluble *adj.*—able to be dissolved in something else. *Example*: Salt is <u>soluble</u> in water.

species *n.*—a group of organisms that can mate and have offspring.

survive *v.*—to live on despite tough circumstances. The theory of evolution is based on "survival of the fittest." That means the organisms best equipped to live in a particular habitat will <u>survive</u> and have offspring.

texture *n.*—the feel of a surface. *Example*: Paper has a smooth <u>texture</u>. Sandpaper has a rough <u>texture</u>.

theory *n.*—a proposed reason why something is what it is. *Example*: Kevin's <u>theory</u> that the sun was a big, glowing breath mint was interesting, but wrong.

thrive *v.*—in science, it means to do really, really well in its habitat. See the definition for *survive*. <u>Thriving</u> is even better than *surviving*!

traits *n.*—the characteristics that make something unique.

transfer *v.*—to pass on. *Example*: In science, parents <u>transfer</u> traits to their offspring.

vapor *n.*—gas formed from something that is usually a liquid.

Notes/Words

Use these pages for the exercises or to write down words
your student is having trouble with that aren't in this book.

Notes/Words

Also Available

20-Minute Learning Connection:
New York Elementary School Edition

Crusade in the Classroom:
How George W. Bush's Education Reforms
Will Affect Your Children, Our Schools

**Parent's Guide to New York State
4th Grade Tests**, Second Edition